Explaining The Presence of God

Peter Rowe

Sovereign World

Bible quotations are taken from
New American Standard Bible © The Lockman Foundation
1960, 1962, 1963, 1968, 1971, 1972, 1973, 1975, 1977.
A Corporation Not for Profit. La Habra, California.

King James Version – Crown copyright.

ISBN: 1 85240 159 1

SOVEREIGN WORLD LIMITED
P.O. Box 777, Tonbridge, Kent TN11 9XT, England.

Typeset and printed in the UK by Sussex Litho Ltd, Chichester, West Sussex.

About the Author

In the early 80s, Peter Rowe was one of the co-founders of Christian City Church, Sydney, under the leadership of Phil Pringle. The church is now a dynamic movement with more than sixty churches worldwide.

Peter has had fifteen years Bible college ministry experience and has also pioneered successful churches and co-founded a Christian primary school, now one of the largest and most highly regarded in Sydney.

In 1987 Peter, his wife and their two children came to Great Britain to establish Christian City Church Europe. He became and remains a lecturer in core subjects at Kensington Temple's 'International Bible Institute of London'. In 1993 he left CCC to set up Metropolitan College of Ministry in central London.

He has a powerful ministry and a God-given ability to release the tangible presence of God.

Dedication

To my friend and mentor, Phil Pringle.

Acknowledgements

Thanks to Joy Hackett for her labour of love,
typing and numerous retypings,
to Marion Osgood and Chris Denne for their
welcome comments and suggestions,
and to Colin Dye, Shakti Sosida, Grenville Barber
and Susan Kerr for their encouragement.

Contents

Introduction

The Presence of God is for Everyone

As we embark upon the last few years of this final decade of the millennium, it is a real joy to hear of worldwide spiritual stirrings. There is a widespread belief in the church that we are entering the final, last days' outpouring of the Holy Spirit which will bring millions into the kingdom of God and herald the return of Jesus. There is a desperate hunger in the people of God for a deep and genuine experience of His presence and power. We have seen evidence of this as large numbers flock to churches where outpourings of the Holy Spirit are being experienced.

It is sad that many are criticised for their 'herd' instincts, or for being thrill-seekers or spiritual freeloaders. Those who step out of conformity to reach out to God have always been criticised. If a blind man named Bartimaeus had listened to others he would never have been healed. The disciples considered the presence of God an adults-only 'production' when they rebuked parents who were bringing their children to Jesus. There were always queues and throngs around Jesus, and there always will be.

People have an innate hunger for the presence of God. They have been 'programmed' that way by the God who made them – *'He has also set eternity in their hearts'* (Ecclesiastes 3:11).

This is a book about entering the presence of God. It is written in the belief that God wants us to experience Him and satisfy the hunger in our hearts. He is a personal and knowable God. Whether we meet with Him in the 'throngs' or in the stillness of our own place of prayer, He waits for us.

The steps that follow in this book are tried and tested. There is a way of entering into God's presence that is for everyone, not just the 'super-spirituals'. Each of us desires a closer relationship with God. I assure you, climbing the stairway to heaven is much easier than it seems.

1

Beginnings

My quest for the presence of God

I was a new believer, enthusiastic and ready to go to the ends of the earth, if that was what the Lord wanted. My conversion to Christ was genuine, I was thrilled to know Him and had a real joy. Yet something was missing!

Even as a child I believed in God, but church was the most uninspiring place to be. I had an emptiness. Knowing about Jesus was not enough. I did not expect to see Him with my physical eyes, but even at that tender age I desired some awareness of God's presence. Like many other young people I left the church as soon as my parents stopped taking me.

During my teens and twenties I continued to believe that God existed but had no idea where or who He was. I tried various religions and philosophies briefly, but found them either too oppressive or philosophically unappealing. In fact, I decided I just didn't have what it took to be religious. One religion wanted me to clear my mind while another offered ridiculous ritual or ascetic fanaticism. I was quite relieved at the age of 31 when receiving Jesus as Lord and Saviour to find that Jesus was God after all – not those ugly idols, rules and regulations or 'experience for the sake of it' fabrications – but was I to accept that going to church, praying, witnessing and being a good person was all there was? Should I forgo my desire to experience God? Maybe it was selfish anyway!

The dilemma didn't stay for long. A friend gave me a copy of Merlin Carothers' book 'Prison to Praise'. What an eye opener! Speaking in tongues, experiencing the presence of God and walking in a close faith-filled relationship with Him; this is it, at last!

I soon found an Assemblies of God church where, they assured me, tongues were spoken. My wife and I joined immediately. The presence of God was real, almost tangible. I began to seek the baptism in the Holy Spirit. I went out for prayer so many times, I'm sure my hair began to wear out from all the laying on of hands, but to no avail. Merlin Carothers had taught that I needed to receive the baptism by faith, and speak in tongues believing I had received – so I did a 'deal' with God: that I would receive by next Sunday, at the latest.

At the church prayer meeting the following Sunday I felt a deep surge of emotion and almost wept, but no tongues. That same evening at home, while my wife was in the dining room with a friend, I sat on my bed determined to receive by faith. Opening my mouth I began to make sounds similar to the ones I had heard people speak in church; I felt silly in my own presence but remember saying in my heart, 'I believe this is from God,' over and over. Within a minute or so a surge of Holy Spirit power flowed through me and the empty sounds I was making became full of faith and content. In an instant I was singing in the spirit, making melodies while waves of the Holy Spirit flowed through and around me. This was ecstasy, a glorious experience of God's presence, yet not at all selfish or sensation-seeking, just pure and holy worship of the living God.

The initial experience of my baptism in the Holy Spirit lasted for about a month in its fullness. I remember one day when I was mopping a floor, the urge to worship came upon me. I had to kneel right then, I couldn't resist, so down I went in all the soap suds and lifted my hands in adoration as more waves of the Holy Spirit filled the atmosphere around me.

My AOG church only had one service and it was in the morning, which simply wasn't enough. Rather than satisfying my hunger, the baptism in the Holy Spirit had only increased my desire to enter the presence of God. In the evenings I used to drive to another AOG church in a neighbouring suburb. It was here that I discovered new dimensions of worship. They would sing in tongues and the weight of God's presence would manifest to such an extent it was almost too much to bear. As I have often said, if I had dropped a pin it would have floated to the ground before being heard. The worship went on and on and on. It was wonderful!

These experiences occurred 20 years ago and I still remember them vividly, even though much greater things have happened since. This hunger for God's presence which began even before I was saved has never left me. This is not to say I haven't been through some extremely 'dry' patches; yet today as I write I am more desperate to dwell in the presence of Almighty God than ever before.

God's presence is addictive, but it is the best addiction a human being can have. It is also a vital requirement for any form of ministry or service as the following pages will reveal. My emphasis on God's presence in no way minimises my faith in the Bible, in fact, the very thesis of this book is to approach the word of God through the 'eyes' of the Spirit.

This book has been written from an earnest desire to teach and encourage God's people to dwell in His presence, to live in the spirit. The Lord has blessed me with an ability to release His 'tangible' presence to a small gathering or to thousands of people. It is my prayer that as you read this book you will receive an anointing that will enable you to experience this abiding presence in every part of your life.

The contents of this book were first preached as a series of messages to a central London church in 1994. Shortly afterwards a well known prophetic minister brought a word from the Lord that I should write a book. This is that book.

2

The Reality of God's Presence

God has substance; He is personal, knowable, tangible

One of the foremost reasons for the creation of man was so he could enjoy living in the presence of God. Some have suggested that man was created by a lonely God for 'fellowship' – but the very nature of God is such that He is self-sufficient, having no needs. Only a God who has no needs can receive worship and be glorified without becoming some form of egotistical despot. God is free from self and able to focus all His attention upon His creatures; thus His love is perfect.

God is a person. The Bible tells us that He has the elements of personality – mind, will and emotions. We are made in the image of God, so like Him we can reason, decide, and feel our emotional responses.

Notwithstanding the incarnation of Jesus, God is Spirit (John 4:24) existing in three persons, Father, Son and Holy Spirit. The three are one and perfectly equal – it is a mystery to us but a biblical fact. Though God is Spirit He is not an ethereal vapour, He is real, tangible, and has form (John 5:37). His presence is powerful, glorious and revelatory. He is Almighty God!

We are spiritual beings

We are also first spirit beings, made in His image, though our spirit is housed in a body of flesh. Thus we have two sets of senses, those relating to our body, and those relating to our spirit.

We do not perceive God with our physical senses (John 4:24) nor can we even understand Him. The Bible tells us that the things of God are foolish to our flesh (1 Corinthians 2:14). How important then that we allow the life in the spirit to predominate.

One of the greatest charges against the church is hypocrisy, and the sad thing is that it is largely true. So often we fail to live in the spirit realm that God purposed as our place of dwelling; a life in the flesh is no witness to an unbeliever.

Of course you can experience God with your physical senses if the Lord decides to meet you that way. Many of our favourite Bible characters, Moses, Joshua, Gideon, Paul and others, have experienced the visual presence of God in various manifestations and many Christians have for example heard God's audible voice or seen say, an angel, with their natural eyes. I have not yet experienced God that way, though I would dearly love to. But I do experience the tangible weight of God's presence on a daily basis.

It seems very hard for us to understand that we are first spiritual beings. Just as we need to learn about and understand the physical realm and environment to live and prosper in our natural surroundings, we need even more to learn about and understand the spiritual realm in order to live in our spiritual environment.

When we feel the presence of God, we lift our hands; sometimes we wave them in the spirit. This is our spirit man expressing himself through our physical being. Peter speaks of the *'hidden person of the heart'* (1 Peter 3:4). It is interesting in the story of the rich man and Lazarus (Luke 16:19-31) that each appeared to be of the same size, shape and appearance as in their physical past. This indicates that our spiritual man is a replica of our outward form, which could explain why we seem to 'feel' God's presence. It is actually our spirit that reaches out for the touch of God, it is our spirit man that falls 'under the power' taking our physical bodies with it.

Where is our memory stored?

I have always been fascinated by the implication of another aspect of the story of the rich man and Lazarus. If, as we are led to believe, all our memory is stored in the brain then how did this rich man remember who Lazarus was or that he had left family behind? Just as the biblical truth of final judgment demands a continuation of memory beyond the grave, there is also a need for believers to remember the character development and experiences of this life in order to perpetuate the lessons learned into eternity. It is clear that our thinking processes and memory go beyond the physical, and that it is in the unseen part of man where our 'hard disc' information base is found.

All people are spiritual

Our spirit man is much more active and real than we often imagine. We suffer a misunderstanding when we say that the spirit of a non-believer is 'dead', presuming it therefore inactive. Nothing could be further from the truth. All human beings are first spiritual, but those who are outside of Christ are 'dead' in the sense of comprehension of, or relationship to, God. Their spirit man is given over to the physical senses; but the spirit of the believer is born again to new life in God. The new birth brings the life of God to our spirit and makes us a new creation in Christ Jesus.

The experience of the presence of God is the most wonderful privilege it is possible for a human being to have – far surpassing any pleasure or experience to be found on earth. There is peace and fullness of joy in God's presence. It is the starting place for all spiritual life, for us who believe, it is 'home'.

You cannot divorce God from His presence any more than you can experience my presence without me. The presence of God is not just a feeling, nor is it like a fragrance that can be enjoyed at a distance from a flower. The presence of God is God Himself; His presence has substance. All spirit has substance – the spirit realm is very real, there is a whole world around us that we cannot actually see, but it is real.

People who hallucinate through drugs and alcohol think they are having bad dreams when really they have artificially induced their inner man to become spiritually aware of the fallen spiritual realm. It is a deceptive realm, like everything the devil has to offer, sometimes beautiful at first but always eventually ugly and terrifying.

As believers, we can move in the unfallen spiritual realm. A realm of beauty and revelation, of perfection and holiness. This realm is also around us all the time but sadly, to many, it is not known and not experienced.

Yes, God's presence has content and substance, but how do we relate this to the fact that He is omnipresent? The most straightforward answer would be that while He is everywhere, He does not manifest His full presence or substance everywhere. When I walk alone in a park I do not go around talking to trees, so I am not manifesting as much of myself as I would if I were surrounded by friends. God is a person too. He only reveals Himself to His people and He is only really substantially revealed when He is around friends. It is wonderful to be a friend of God!

The weight of God's presence

The presence of God also has weight. When the glory of God came into Solomon's temple the priests could not even stand up. It would have been fascinating to see them in their festal robes, laying on the floor totally incapable of rising or lifting any part of their bodies. Can you imagine the worship coming from their mouths as they glorified God?

The Bible speaks of an eternal weight of glory (2 Corinthians 4:17). We feel the weight of God's presence in varying ways but particularly during strong silences when the presence of God is heavy, sometimes so heavy it seems to take our breath away. The phenomenon of going down 'under the power' or as some call it 'slain in the spirit' is also related to the weight of glory. In these days we are experiencing some wonderful moves of God's Spirit in the churches but relative to what has been seen in by-gone revivals, and what God can and will do in the future, it is only a drop in the ocean.

When we begin to move in a fuller, stronger weight of God's presence we will begin to see more of His attributes and manifestations. It's all fairly 'safe' at the moment, but the same outpouring that brought incredible miracles in the early church also brought judgment upon Ananias and Sapphira.

A sense of the fear of God has been missing from the Church

in this age. Everyone talks about it, preachers expound it from the pulpit, but we can't fake the fear of God any more than we can enter some of the deep levels of repentance and unity that many leaders attempt to draw us into without a move of God's Spirit. When God begins to move in exceptional ways we will begin to see exceptional things. Nevertheless, we can begin to move into the presence of God as individuals and churches. I believe God has an open door before each one of us, a window of opportunity in the spirit. I strongly believe this book will quicken your spirit to go through.

> *'Seek the Lord while He may be found;*
> *Call upon Him while He is near.'*   (Isaiah 55:6)

A fuller weight of God's glory will revolutionise the Church. Power and revelation will flow, signs and wonders will abound, multitudes will be saved. Yet as we have seen with Ananias and Sapphira, the glory of God will also reveal His judgments. This will occur because of a more complete manifestation of God's attributes. Our God is a Consuming Fire; He is holy and awesome. In the limited manifestations of God that we have at present, people have behaved irreverently, and got away with it. They will not escape retribution, unless of course they repent, but it happens more slowly. When the weight of glory comes, the fear of God comes too; judgments are swift, but then so are miracles.

In the Scriptures we see God's awesome power revealed. The dead are raised, plagues are sent, mighty miracles are witnessed, and angelic visitations are received. It's amazing that the 'nice' feeling we get in church is the presence of the living God! The Bible tells us that at His presence:

- Sinai quaked
- mountains melted like wax
- the earth and all its people will shake
- roads will collapse
- the universe flees

What a mighty God we serve! It would take billions of years for us to cross His universe at the speed of light (186,000 miles per second). Many of the stars we see are entire solar systems billions of miles across. However big the universe is, it is no more than a speck under the fingernail of our infinite eternal God.

3

The Content of God's Presence

A heavenly realm. Angels, glory and blessings

'The angel of His presence saved them.' (Isaiah 63:9)

The presence of God contains a whole spiritual realm with mighty angels. When Elisha was surrounded by a great army of Arameans his servant was perplexed at the calmness of his master, saying *'Alas, my master! What shall we do?'* (2 Kings 6:15). The answer came from this great prophet who clearly had a deep understanding of the realm of the spirit and the presence of God:

> *'So he answered "Do not fear, for those who are with us are more than those who are with them." Then Elisha prayed and said, "O Lord, I pray, open his eyes that he may see." And the Lord opened the servant's eyes, and he saw; and behold, the mountain was full of horses and chariots of fire all around Elisha.'* (2 Kings 6:16-17)

Jacob, having seen a vision of a stairway going straight into heaven with the Lord above it and angels ascending and descending on it exclaimed, *'This is none other than the house of God...'* The house of God is not a church building, it is the place where His presence dwells. The angelic vision was part of the spiritual content of the presence of God.

There are always angels in the presence of God. Isaiah saw seraphim in a vision of the Lord in the temple (Isaiah 6). The way to the presence of God (the tree of life) was blocked by cherubim (Genesis 3:24) and of course the cherubim woven into the veil of the tabernacle and the temple and moulded into the mercy seat were representations of a spiritual reality (Exodus 36:8).

Angels

The study of angels is really exciting; some are massive, possibly bigger than the earth! No, I'm not trying to shock you or to be controversial. In the book of Revelation (10:2) a huge angel is mentioned who has one foot in the sea and another on the land. Presuming this angel was not paddling at Brighton, I can only assume that it must be several miles high! Other angels in Scripture appear to be the same size as men, while still others are noted for their strength and power.

We have the idea that angels are of human size with a pair of wings on their backs. The cherub must be the most misrepresented of all angels, usually being depicted as about the size of a toddler with a cute little backside and a pair of small wings, probably holding a small harp or a bow and arrow. Nothing could be further from the truth. The cherubim in Ezekiel have four faces and four wings with four legs like calves, gleaming as burnished bronze. They each had human hands and of the four faces, one was like that of a man, one, a lion, one, a bull, one, an eagle. Each also had four front sides, they never turned, so whichever direction they went they could go forward, always in response to the Holy Spirit. Finally each had a wheel which worked with the wheel of another, a bit like a gyroscope. Each of the wheels were full of eyes all around and from their midst came a fire like burning coals (Ezekiel 1).

It sounds quite frightening but the Scriptures tell us these creatures are perfect in beauty (Ezekiel 28:12 cf 14). We will not fear them because they are beautiful to behold and because we are saved. It is worth noting that Satan was one of these creatures but fell from grace and beauty (Ezekiel 28:16). The creatures in Isaiah chapter 6 and Revelation chapter 1 are called seraphim and are equally awesome in appearance, although it is possible that not all cherubim and seraphim look the same. The realm of the spirit where angels dwell is amazing and exciting. We have some powerful allies; praise the Lord!

There are blessings in His presence

The Scriptures tell us so much about the content of God's

presence. There are many blessings available to us:

Direction   God's will is revealed to us in His presence. It is
              clear direction, not guesswork (Numbers 16:6-7).

Prophecy   Powerful prophecy is released in the presence of
              the Lord (Jeremiah 17:16).

Revelation   God's word releases revelation to us. We are
              exhorted to 'eat' in His presence (Deuteronomy
              14:23 cf 8:3).

Joy   His presence fills us with gladness (Isaiah 9:3,
              Acts 2:28).

Refreshment   God's presence always brings refreshment; it is
              never stale (Acts 3:19).

Exaltation   James promises exaltation when we humble
              ourselves in God's presence. The prominence we
              need to make an impact comes from the presence
              of God, not man-made promotion (James 4:10 cf
              Joshua 3:7).

Rest   *'Cease striving and know that I am God,'* says
              the Psalmist (Psalm 46:10). As we enter into
              God's presence we step into the wonderful world
              of His rest (Exodus 33:14).

Help   *'Hope in God, for I shall again praise Him For
              the help of His presence,'* (Psalm 42:5).

The Scriptures also reveal many other wonderful things that are
found in God's presence. It is the source of healing, prosperity,
power and all blessing. In fact, blessing can only really be given
from the source of God's presence; it is an impartation of real
spiritual substance (Genesis 27:7; 27:33-35). Decide now to be a
minister of blessing.

Relationship with God

The most wonderful thing about abiding in the presence of God is
not the blessings we receive but the close relationship we develop
with Him.

The Holy Spirit

After He rose from the dead, Jesus sent the Holy Spirit. One of the roles of the Holy Spirit is to bring the presence of God and to reveal and glorify God the Father, and Jesus, God the Son. It is impossible to have a relationship with someone you don't know. One difficulty I had as a new believer was in trying to locate three different members of the Godhead in prayer and worship. In fact it got quite confusing. Then the Lord spoke to my heart: 'Those that worship me must worship me in spirit' – I then realized that my first relationship was to be with the Holy Spirit and through that relationship I would develop knowledge and closeness with the Father and the Son. I remembered the blessings at the end of some of the New Testament books: *'The grace of the Lord Jesus Christ, and the love of God, and the fellowship of the Holy Spirit, be with you all.'* Yes, fellowship with the Holy Spirit. The Holy Spirit is the member of the Godhead who works with people. Jesus rose and sent Another; the Holy Spirit is now our Emmanuel, God with us. This does not diminish Jesus because the role of the Holy Spirit is to glorify Him, to draw attention to Him. Once I am filled with the Holy Spirit my heart reaches out in praise to Jesus – but my point here is that we must have a relationship with the Holy Spirit first.

Sin keeps man out of God's presence

Adam had a relationship with God. He walked with God every day. He enjoyed a wonderful level of verbal communication. God wanted Adam to stay in His presence for ever, but we all know what happened – sin got in the way. Immediately Adam sinned he lost his relationship with God. He knew that he had done wrong and felt guilty, so he hid himself in the garden (Genesis 3:8).

Something in our innate sense of justice makes us avoid people we have wronged – possibly it is the fear of retribution. Nowhere in the narrative does it say that God avoided Adam; in fact He arrived at the usual time for His walk in the garden – it was Adam who withdrew from God.

We know that unbelievers cannot enjoy God's presence because of their sin, but it is sad that believers so often hide away simply because, like Adam, they feel unworthy, guilty.

Old Testament believers thought that they would die if they saw the Lord, so they feared His presence. Moses looked away from the burning bush when he heard God speak. Gideon was afraid when he discovered the angel he was speaking to was God Himself, but the Lord assured him, saying, *'Peace to you, do not fear; you shall not die'* (Judges 6:23). Even the mighty prophet Isaiah, as he saw a vision of God in all His glory, did not fall down and worship, but instead cried aloud, *'Woe is me, for I am ruined! Because I am a man of unclean lips'* (Isaiah 6:5).

I will return to the subject of guilt soon, but first I want to mention that the cross of Jesus Christ made a path for us right into the presence of God. The writer of Hebrews exhorts us to *'draw near with confidence to the throne of grace'* (Hebrews 4:16). Paul says we have already been raised up with Him, and are seated with him in the heavenly places in Christ Jesus (Ephesians 2:6). Isn't this wonderful news? We are already seated at the right hand of the Majesty on high with Jesus! It is so exciting – yet sadly most believers do not enter into God's presence, let alone rule with Him from the throne of heaven. We consistently seem to fall short of the New Testament norm.

God desires to lift us into new heights in our Christian walk. Let your faith and expectancy rise up as you read this book. You will be wonderfully surprised!

4

Alone with God

The real test, winning over the flesh

There are two arenas for enjoying the presence of God. Firstly, with other believers. Secondly, when you are alone with God.

God's presence corporately

For those who attend Pentecostal or Charismatic churches the tangible presence of God during praise, worship and ministry should be a regular experience. There are however, varying degrees of intensity. For instance, I have led meetings where the heavy presence of God has reduced us to total silence for lengthy periods.

Some time ago, during my years as a pastor in West London, I was leading our Friday evening prayer meeting. All our prayer meetings were marked by the tangible presence of God but this one was different. The power of God fell, bringing a powerful silence. It was a stillness that could be felt. An hour went by as if it were five minutes. It was tinged with a genuine fear of God. We were reluctant to move, even to get comfortable, lest we disturb His presence. Not one prayer was prayed, no Scripture was read nor one song sung; our lips remained silent. After an hour the presence of the Holy Spirit lifted enough for us to tiptoe to our cars. We had met with God.

I have also seen people falling spontaneously under the power of God at random throughout a congregation. Sometimes there is a move of extreme joy when people fall down laughing, while others weep. There are many other manifestations, but it is the same Spirit.

It is very easy to enjoy the presence of God when we are all together. It is possible for someone, who alone may have little relationship with God, to come into a good church service and flow in His presence, fall under the power, prophesy or even preach – only to return home to a dry, frustrating, unproductive spiritual life.

One of the reasons for this is that God's presence is released in a very special way when we gather together: '*For where two or three have gathered together in My name, there I am in their midst*' (Matthew 18:20).

It is not some sort of group dynamic like at a football match or a political rally; it is God; God with His people. There is great power in our unity in Christ but it is a power in the spirit; not some soulish imitation. It is holy.

> '*Behold, how good and how pleasant it is*
> *For brothers to dwell together in unity!*
> *It is like the precious oil upon the head,*
> *Coming down upon the beard,*
> *Even Aaron's beard,*
> *Coming down upon the edge of his robes.*
> *It is like the dew of Hermon,*
> *Coming down upon the mountains of Zion;*
> *For there the Lord commanded the blessing – life forever.*'
>   (Psalm 133)

Our times together present great opportunities to build the presence of God for our private devotions. The Israelites gathered the manna and took it home. God's presence accumulates. There is a need to capitalize on powerful times of corporate praise, worship and prayer. Whenever the weight of God's presence is upon us, our spiritual awareness is heightened and our spiritual faculties lubricated. These are God-given opportunities that enable us to go deeper into the spirit when alone with Him. It is a waste when we squander our spiritual highs on worldly pursuits. It is not good practice when climbing high on the 'stairway', to 'unwind' by, for instance, watching TV. It is a sad indictment on human nature that having got to the top of the 'mountain' we are in such a hurry to climb down.

Many years ago, a great man of God, who had a mighty

preaching and miracle ministry, 'unwound' after the meetings with a glass of whiskey. This man, who had pre-Christian problems with drink, felt invincible because he was filled with the Holy Spirit. His one drink became two, then three, then the whole bottle! He became an alcoholic and his ministry floundered.

The confidence we gain when in the spirit can, paradoxically, make us vulnerable to the things of the flesh. The Bible reveals that spiritual intoxication can be mistaken for drunkenness (Acts 2:15). We are encouraged not to get drunk with wine but rather with the Holy Spirit (Ephesians 5:18). The closer we get to God the greater the responsibility to stay away from the 'world' and its enticements. This is the cost of remaining in the presence of God; a price that is far outweighed by the blessings we receive.

Alone with God

For many of us the most challenging time of all is in our private devotions — the time when we wrestle with the flesh and if we were to be honest, sometimes lose. The less time we spend with God, the harder it gets. We all know how hard it is to win back a prayer habit that has been lost on the altar of tiredness, guilt, laziness, or a variety of other 'reasons'.

You can enjoy the presence of God at home, or out walking, or virtually anywhere, without having other believers prime the pump for you. God's presence is for ordinary people like you and me, not a special bonus for the 'super-spiritual'. I would go further and say that the most spiritual people I know are the most down-to-earth.

An example of this is a very human seventeenth-century monk, Brother Lawrence, who discovered how to delight in the presence of God amongst the clatter and clutter of a busy monastic kitchen. Even though written almost three hundred years ago by a French Catholic mystic, his writings, collected under the title 'The Practice of the Presence of God,'[1] are held in high esteem and form one of the great spiritual classics. Though it needs to be

[1]Brother Lawrence, The Practice of the Presence of God. Trans., E.M. Blaiklock. London: Hodder and Stoughton, 1981.

understood in its Catholic, monastic context, it is still a deeply rewarding book to read.

Let us look now at some common hindrances to entering into the presence of God as well as related remedies. This will give us a clean slate for Chapter 5 when we take serious steps into the glory of God.

Five major hindrances

1. Guilt

I am sure this is our biggest hindrance. It presents us with a mindset that is hard to break unless we apply the word of God boldly to our lives. It is the same problem we saw with Adam, Moses, Gideon and Isaiah in Chapter 3, except we have Jesus. The problem is that our flesh has trouble accepting the work of the Cross, particularly when we feel bad about ourselves.

How is it that Moses feared for his life when he stood on holy ground, but David didn't turn a hair when unlawfully eating consecrated bread (Matthew 12:3-4)? We know that David's 'sin' was not held against him because of faith.

> *'My righteous one shall live by faith; and if he shrinks back, my soul has no pleasure in him.'*   (Hebrews 10:38)

Jesus paid the price for every sin at Calvary so we are forgiven, even for sins that recur, if we look to the cross. All sins are forgiven as we put our faith in Jesus. Remember, it was Adam who moved away, not God. God will not leave you, His presence is there to be enjoyed.

> *'I will never desert you, nor will I ever forsake you.'*
>   (Hebrews 13:5)

If God can forget our sins then maybe we ought to do the same. Once you get close to Him on a regular basis you will experience more and more victory. The desire to sin will diminish as you gain the upper hand over the flesh through your new found closeness to God.

I have learned how to stand on the 'word' and receive forgiveness for sins but there are other more subtle things that can arise as I seek God. Things like, 'I haven't prayed enough this week' or a harsh word given or received. On occasions I have spent much of my prayer time rehearsing an argument or thinking about a hurtful thing someone has said to me. There are so many things that make us feel guilty.

We can somehow avoid guilt feelings when we go to church and enjoy our corporate blessing but when we stand before the Lord alone it can be as if a door has been closed before us.

A simple but powerful solution for guilt is to confess it as sin. The Bible says whatever is not from faith is sin (Romans 14:23). Confess your sin then step through it into the presence of God. If you have confessed and received forgiveness, it is dealt with! Now this does not mean that when you step out of your prayer closet you can ignore the consequences of sin, but you will have new power to do the right thing.

Remember we do not come to God on the basis of yesterday's prayer time or how many people we have witnessed to, but on the basis of faith.

2. Laziness

'The spirit is willing but the flesh is weak' are familiar words to all of us. I have been privileged to meet some of the finest men and women of God on the face of the earth and many of them would admit that they struggle to get motivated in prayer.

I wish I could say that confessing laziness as sin would take it away, but *'faith without works is dead.'* Laziness is lethargy. It has no momentum and the only way to overcome it is to tackle it head on.

Laziness and its 'soul-mate' procrastination are often the product of fear or a poor self-image. Teachers often put off preparing lectures to avoid confronting the fear of delivery. I know! If you have a problem with laziness because of fear, or fear of failure, or feelings of inadequacy, or inferiority, talk to someone about it, or better still, talk to God – that is what He is there for.

Having seriously looked for underlying causes it is time to confront. Make a decision and declare it to God, to seek Him daily, regularly and aggressively. Before long you will be wondering whatever kept you away.

One of the major problems with laziness is that it racks people with guilt. All lazy people feel guilty about it and of course this further separates them from God. *'Arise, O man of God'* – make an unbreakable decision; ask the Holy Spirit to help. *'...The kingdom of heaven suffers violence, and violent men take it by force'* (Matthew 11:12).

3. Lack of spiritual hunger

Fasting, with its denial of physical appetite, is often followed by lack of hunger. It is then necessary to retrain the appetite by building it up with small amounts of nutritional food to regain strength and normal hunger patterns. Our spirit needs building up with real spiritual food so our hunger can develop:

> *'Man does not live on bread alone, but on every word that proceeds out of the mouth of God.'*   (Matthew 4:4)

Our spiritual food is the word of God and prayer and fellowship with other believers. It may take courage to eat your first meal; I can't even promise that you will enjoy it, but I guarantee you will be strengthened spiritually and that your hunger will develop after a while.

Speaking in tongues is a major stimulant to spiritual hunger. Speak in tongues boldly for just five minutes and you will want to carry on.

Get serious with God, tell Him you are fed-up with being spiritually dull and want to be on fire for Him. He really cares, He does answer prayer and He will help. Over to you!

4. Pre-occupation

The wandering mind syndrome can be a real problem when you want to get moving with God. I think television is part of the problem. We are so used to being fed information and entertainment in bite-size chunks that we expect every area of life to be user-friendly, or else we lose concentration.

It is important to remember that the things of God are not trivial. I am sure that you could find a cartoon version of the Bible somewhere but I am not sure that it would feed your spirit. Trivial things require trivial effort but the things of God, like anything important in life, require commensurate effort. We have already seen that laziness is no excuse. Read the book of Proverbs and find out what God thinks of it:

> *'A little sleep, a little slumber,*
> *A little folding of the arms to rest –*
> *And your poverty will come in like a vagabond,*
> *And your need like an armed man.'*　　　(Proverbs 6:10-11)

Our flesh will always go for what comes easiest, is most immediately interesting, or consumes our thoughts. God wants our full attention.

Each time we begin to pray and seek God a war breaks out. Our flesh wars against our spirit and our spirit wars against our flesh. What ensues is a spiritual wrestling match, often precipitated by spiritual enemies who seek to fill our minds with thoughts not conducive to seeking God. Every time we pray we need to put the flesh to death and get the enemy on the run. Instead, we so often take the easy route and give in. Ask yourself – 'What am I made of? Am I a warrior, bringing down the strongholds of Satan, or am I the devil's doormat?'

If you had an audience with the Queen, you would not come before her thinking about the groceries or your favourite hobby or what is on TV; you would be consumed with the honour of being in her presence. Yet we stand in the presence of God and think about anything rather than Him, just because He is not visible. Many Christians would sooner read the back of a cornflakes packet than the Bible. No wonder our untrained minds lose concentration. The Scriptures encourage us to set our minds on the things above (Colossians 3:2). At Metropolitan College of Ministry we have Scripture Memory in the curriculum. This is not made into a chore – just two verses a week for the duration of the course. It is absolutely amazing the difference it makes to the students when they get the word of God on the inside of them.

I strongly urge you to get hold of some blank cards and write out your favourite verses. Why not try just one a week. It will make such a difference.

> *'And do not be conformed to this world, but be transformed by the renewing of your mind ...'*　　　　(Romans 12:2)

I teach my students about focus. In prayer and praise our words and vision are very powerful. We would not take a gun and fire it blindly into the air hoping it will hit the target. We aim carefully, put our finger on the trigger and fire. Focus is like that – we take every ounce of spiritual energy we can muster, aim it at the target of prayer, or warfare, or releasing God's presence, and fire with faith and energy. We hit the target, we become skilful and we start to enjoy what we are doing because the haphazard element is gone. By controlling our focus we have also brought our thoughts into line.

On a last practical note, keep a notepad with you when you pray. If you think of something important, write it down, then you can forget about it.

5. Lack of expectation

I am sure this book will address the problem of low expectation by raising your expectation levels to new heights.

This problem is closely related to doubt, when someone simply does not expect to experience the presence of God. Nevertheless, I am not saying that God will not do anything unless we expect it. He is full of surprises!

At Bethesda Jesus once healed a cripple who had less faith in his whole body than most of you have in your big toe. Elijah was so 'burnt out' that he sat under a tree in the desert and hoped to die. Instead he had angelic visitations, a miraculous 600-mile walk and a mind-boggling mountaintop experience with God.

Many times I have come out of a hard grinding hour of prayer and just when I am ready for a coffee and off to work, the power of God falls. It makes you feel like saying, 'Where were you when I needed you?' Of course, this last minute manifestation is a confirmation. It means you have taken the ground from the enemy and raised the flag of Jesus Christ; you have taken a position. I have learned not to walk out at times like this; they are very special. I just enjoy His presence for another five minutes or so. I get a real kick out of spending a little more time with God than I planned.

Most often when I am in prayer I expect God to manifest His presence. I begin to see the spirit realm around me, first by thinking about it – for instance, John's vision of the throne of God in Revelation, or Elisha's chariots of fire. This is an act of faith that opens up the realm of the spirit. I am going to look more closely at this in later chapters, but it is of paramount importance that our spiritual eyes are open when we desire to enter God's presence. The realm of the spirit is so exciting!

> *'In the year of King Uzziah's death, I saw the Lord sitting on a throne, lofty and exalted, with the train of His robe filling the temple. Seraphim stood above Him, each having six wings; with two he covered his face, and with two he covered his feet, and with two he flew. And one called out to another and said, "Holy, Holy, Holy, is the Lord of hosts, The whole earth is full of His glory." And the foundations of the thresholds trembled at the voice of him who called out, while the temple was filling with smoke.'* (Isaiah 6:1-4)

5

A Biblical Pattern

God of the universe who lets me come near

Ezekiel is the prophet we associate with the glory of God. He had such wonderful experiences in the presence of the Lord. Once he was given a prophetic vision of the temple that will be built in Jerusalem after the second coming of Christ (chapter 47). He was led to a river that came forth from the Holy of Holies, the inner chamber. The river represents the presence of God. Ezekiel was led to go deeper and deeper until all he could do was swim.

As long as Ezekiel waded in the waters he could stand on his own two feet. He was in control. But in order to swim in the depths of the river he had to take his feet off the ground, putting his entire trust in the waters. Ask anyone who is learning to swim what is the hardest part and they will always say taking their feet off the bottom and trusting in the buoyancy of the water.

Our pattern for entering God's presence is found in the first two verses of Psalm 63 which we will look at in its progressive parts:

> *'O God, Thou art my God; I shall seek Thee earnestly;*
> *My soul thirsts for Thee, my flesh yearns for Thee,*
> *In a dry and weary land where there is no water.*
> *Thus I have beheld Thee in the sanctuary,*
> *To see Thy power and Thy glory.'*   (Psalm 63:1-2)

STEP 1 – God (Psalm 63:1)

The first essential is to concentrate upon God rather than our desire for experience. Paul tells us to keep seeking the things above where Christ is (Colossians 3:2). In the Psalms, David actively thought about the works of God in creation:

> *'When I consider Thy heavens, the work of Thy fingers,*
> *The moon and the stars, which Thou hast ordained.'*
>
> (Psalm 8:3)

We have already contemplated the hugeness of God; in fact we will probably never fully comprehend His magnitude. Mary, as her heart turned to God in praise following the annunciation of Jesus' birth, uttered, *'My soul doth magnify the Lord'* (Luke 1:46 KJV).

To magnify is to make bigger; Mary made God bigger in her thoughts following a revelation of God's greatness. As we magnify Him, the more real, great and powerful He becomes to us. We have all heard sermons 'How Big is Your God?' This topic is preached a lot because it is crucial to our Christian life. People who live at a low faith threshold do not have a healthy concept of God's greatness. When Lot was rescued from Sodom, God's saving angels led him to a high mountain, but he declined, pointing instead to a small town called Zoar. *'... This town is near enough to flee to, and it is small. Please, let me escape there (is it not small?)'* (Genesis 19:20).

The name Zoar means 'brought low'. The same expression is used in the story of Gideon when the Israelites hid in dens and caves to escape the Midianites, *'So Israel was brought very low...'* (Judges 6:6). In both cases they had lost their vision of the greatness of God.

In our first step into God's presence we start to think about the different aspects of His greatness – His power, knowledge, love, creativeness, patience and so on, praising Him for all His works just as David did, seeing every other so-called power as a drop in the ocean compared with our Almighty God. Praise is a two-edged sword; one edge gives glory to God, the other reminds us just how wonderful He is. Prayer works in the same way. God does not need to keep hearing but we need to convince ourselves that God has met our need. In the Old Testament they built memorials, piles of stones to remind them and future generations of great deliverances from their enemies. Sometimes they were built to record mighty miracles such as crossing the River Jordan on dry ground; at other times, a visitation of God, such as Jacob had at Bethel. Today we must constantly remind ourselves, through the word of God, through praise and with our words and thoughts that He is God Almighty, Creator of all things.

STEP 2 – You are MY GOD (Psalm 63:1)

Now we turn our thoughts from the God who strung out the planets like pearls on a string to the God we know in a personal way. The God of all creation is not just transcendent but also immanent – not just out there in the vastness of eternity but here with me in my own time and space. He knows me, understands me, He knows the number of hairs on my head. He knows my thoughts even before I think them. He communicates with me; we have a relationship.

God is personal, especially for you and especially for me. I am not just one of the masses who cram into the tube bound for central London each day, I am His child, an individual. It has been said that if you, or I, were the only person alive 2,000 years ago then Jesus would have still gone to the Cross. The wonderful thing about being a Christian is that it gives me value, purpose, a genuine reason for existence. I am both unique and valid. I have 100% of God's attention 24 hours a day!

Who am I?

Moses asked God who He was, and the reply came, '*I am who I am!*' (Exodus 3:14) – no lengthy description, just a simple statement of personal existence.

Many believers spend their lives trying to discover who they really are. Moses, when called to be a deliverer of Israel, replied to the Lord, '*Who am I that I should go to Pharoah?*' People are crying out for identity, for a feeling of self-worth. We tend to identify ourselves by what we do; I do this or I do that, but before I am Principal of Metropolitan College of Ministry I am 'me'. I am different from you, my needs are different, my dreams are

36

different, even my tastes are different. I need to be treated as an individual.

The world tries to put us in a box. People attempt to break out of these imposed 'boxes' by non-conformist behaviour. Fashion dictates the cut of our jacket and the pattern of our ties; so many turn to extremes to be noticed. The cry of the human heart is for acceptance and recognition, to be accepted for who we are. Even the church attempts to put us in boxes with formulae! If you do this, this and this then you will move in my gift, says the preacher. The Bible clearly states that different gifts are for different people; there are varieties of gifts, ministries and effects. You cannot stand in the gift and anointing of Kenneth Hagin, Benny Hinn or Yonggi Cho – no more can they do what you have been called to do.

The real me

Jesus once tested His disciples as to His true identity (Matthew 16:13-17). They offered answers like John the Baptist, Elijah, Jeremiah or one of the prophets. Turning to Peter He received the response, *'Thou art the Christ, the Son of the living God.'* Jesus replied, *'Blessed are you, Simon Barjona because flesh and blood did not reveal this to you, but My Father who is in heaven.'* Following this, Jesus spoke a revelation of personal identity to Peter, *'And I also say to you that you are Peter, and upon this rock I will build My church...'* (v18).

You see, the real person, whether of Jesus or Peter, cannot be revealed by the flesh any more than the real you can be. You are really you when you are in the spirit; when you are in the presence of God. This is when and where God reveals not just Himself to us, but us to ourselves.

> *'And he* (Jacob)[1] *built an altar there, and called the place El Bethel,* (House of God)[1] *because there God had revealed Himself to him.'*   (Genesis 35:7)

[1]Parenthesis mine.

STEP 3 – I SHALL Seek Thee (Psalm 63:1)

To seek God's presence is an act of our will; we have to decide to do so. For me this is the hardest part. When Jesus turned to Peter, James and John saying, *'... the spirit is willing, but the flesh is weak'* (Mark 14:38), I think He was saying it to Himself as much as to them. He was having a huge battle between spirit and flesh and cried to God, *'Yet not what I will, but what Thou wilt'* (v36).

If we can win the battle of the will; then we have won! The enemy will do everything in his power to ensure that our will stays on the flesh side of the equation but to be a seeker of God we have to break out. Our flesh does not want to seek God – it is not even interested! The flesh wants to watch television, sleep, play football or eat. Your spirit is crying out for some spiritual activity.

That wonderful moment when we step out of the flesh into the spirit makes it worth it all. Praise and prayer flows from our innermost being. God's presence is manifested. Revelation comes into our spirit – we are transformed.

Let us agree, let us decide today that we will seek God, whatever our flesh says; whatever Satan says. Let us commit ourselves to seek Him regularly.

> *'When Thou didst say, "Seek My face" my heart said to Thee, "Thy face, O Lord, I shall seek."'* (Psalm 27:8)

6

Seek the Lord

Locating God's presence; digging deep wells

STEP 4 – I Shall SEEK Thee (Psalm 63:1)

Someone once asked me if it was really possible to pray without ceasing. The answer everyone seems to want is, 'No, of course you can't pray all the time'. But it is just not true, we can pray without ceasing.

Ask a person who prays a lot and they will tell you that they are aware of a constant groaning from their spirit towards God. Prayer without ceasing is not saying one prayer after another, it is an ongoing process which ultimately seems involuntary.

We are exhorted to seek God's face continually (I Chronicles 16:11). The experience of continually seeking God is one where we don't have to battle with our will any more because the will doesn't want to stop praying. Isn't it amazing that we can reach a place of total surrender, a place where we can concentrate on God and the needs of others rather than ourselves!

Locate His presence

An intriguing scripture is found in Isaiah 55:6: *'Seek the Lord while He may be found'*. Does this mean that it is easier to find Him at some times than at others? In my experience, yes! I have had seasons in my life when, without any extra effort, the Lord seems incredibly close. Seeking Him in these seasons is so easy. Yet at other times it is such a struggle to hold on to a position in God, it seems to slip through my fingers. I am sure that God makes it harder at times so as to strengthen us spiritually. Then of course, there is the enemy who will do everything in his power to keep us back from God's presence.

There are seasons in the spirit; there is a time to sow and a time to reap. When it is reaping time and God's presence is easy to find, we should labour until the sun goes down. A farmer will work every moment of daylight during harvest time. During times of ploughing and sowing there may seem little reward for the effort, but it will come if we do not grow weary or cease from our labours.

Does God hide?

On occasions I feel so close to God that I never want to 'come down from the mountain'. I have pleaded with God to let me stay and not to take His presence away. I think this is how Peter felt when he suggested building tabernacles on the mount of transfiguration (Mark 9:5). Then suddenly it is over. Where is God? It seems as if He is nowhere to be found and our position has slipped from mountain top to valley.

One minute Moses was on Mount Sinai basking in the glory of God, next he was in the valley rebuking the wicked Israelites and smashing the tablets of the law. Elijah was on top of a mountain, deep in the presence of God, calling down fire from heaven and breaking a three-and-a-half year drought by prayer. Then, in what would seem no time at all, he was in the wilderness beseeching God to take his life. David, during a dark period, cried out to the Lord, *'How long wilt Thou hide Thy face from me?'* (Psalm 13:1).

It is as if God hides himself. He tells us to seek Him, which indicates that He is not always readily found. In Isaiah 45:15 He declares Himself as a *'God who hides Himself'*. How do we find God when He 'hides'? Does He want us to find Him? Yes! Why then does He hide? He wants us to use our spiritual faculties to locate Him in His dwelling place, the spirit realm.

Have you ever been to a church service where there is such an anointing on a song and you sing it over and over again and the power of God falls? 'What a great meeting' everyone says afterwards. Then the following week you do the same thing and it seems as stale as last week's communion bread.

Like the Israelites, we cannot live off yesterday's 'manna'; the presence of God has to be relocated. He may be in praise, He may be in reading the 'word', He may be in 'loud', He may be in 'quiet', He may want you to prophesy or to dance. Wherever God wants us to locate Him, we need to become skilled craftsmen in the spirit.

Once when I was leading a New Year's Eve midnight prayer meeting, I felt in the spirit behind me a massive wave of angelic handclapping. As the wave moved over the stage, we also began to clap with all our might, then starting at the front row and working back about one thousand people joined in the most powerful handclapping of praise I have ever experienced, even to this day. There is an enormous sense of satisfaction when we click in to what the Lord is doing and see such a mighty result.

Have you ever arranged to meet someone at, say, a large railway station and after waiting a long time there is no sign of them, so you leave alone? Later you find out they were there after all. I am sure it is like this with God. Locating God's presence is such an important topic, I want to devote the rest of this chapter to it.

Abraham's wells – Genesis 26:15-18
Just as wells are dug to locate water so we dig spiritual wells to locate the presence of God. Natural life is dependent on water but nowhere is this appreciated more than in dry countries. Spiritual life is dependent upon God's presence, in a *'dry and weary land where there is no water'* (Psalm 63:1). Locating the presence of God is not just a spiritual exercise, it is a matter of spiritual life and death!

We have seen the futility of attempting to live off last week's anointing, but some people try to live off the last move of God! Abraham's wells had been blocked up so that no water could be extracted (v15); yet, *'Isaac dug again the wells of water which had been dug up in the days of his father Abraham ...'* (v18). He even gave them the same names! He really was trying to relive the past.

In the 1970's and 1980's the main criticism of the established church by Pentecostals was that they held to a form of godliness but denied its power (2 Timothy 3:5). Ironically, many of the Pentecostal trappings have now become outward forms themselves. It goes beyond outward form, however. God is doing a new thing in the 1990's. He is restoring prophetic and apostolic ministries and restructuring the Church. It is time for change, time to move on in the spirit. The old wells, like Abraham's, are finished; let us leave the past behind. Those wells were valid in their time and the experiences that flowed helped to shape the things of today, but the wells themselves are full of the desert, empty and dry. There is no life in them.

Living Water

> *'But when Isaac's servants dug in the valley and found there a well of flowing water...'* (Genesis 26:19)

When Isaac moved with God, he dug new wells, and those wells produced, according to the literal Hebrew, 'living water'. This was a bubbling spring or an underground stream. We know from John's gospel that this expression is used to denote the Holy Spirit-filled believer. It is time for all of us to dig into this new move of God's Spirit and allow its life to flow through us.

Conflict

Next the inevitable happened. As soon as the new well was dug there was conflict (Genesis 26:20), but undeterred they kept digging more wells. When we enter into the new move of the Holy Spirit there will be conflict – from the devil, from the world, even from other Christians who complain and criticize, but we must keep pushing on into God. The well was named *Esek* meaning 'contention' or 'accusation'. The devil is the accuser of the brethren and accusation can easily lead to guilt, particularly when we are getting close to God. When I get very close to God the enemy invariably accuses me of pride; it's so plausible that I have often taken it on board. Accusation can sap the joy out of our new found level of relationship. It is at times like this we remind ourselves of Romans 8:1-2 – *'There is therefore now no condemnation for those who are in Christ Jesus. For the law of the Spirit of life in Christ Jesus has set you free from the law of sin and death.'*

The next well produced even more conflict, it was called *Sitna* which comes from the same Hebrew root word as 'Satan'. It was a real spiritual attack, but they were digging into the presence of God and even Satan himself could not stop them. Finally they dug a well where they could find rest from their enemies. This they named *Rehoboth* (v22) which means a 'broad place'.

When we start seeking the presence of God we find it, then lose it, then find it again. We will face conflict and' maybe even discouragement but, if we keep going seeking the Lord, He will eventually bring us to Rehoboth – a broad place, a place of growth, expansion, vision, and fruitfulness. Having established themselves at Rehoboth the Lord led them to dig another well, at Beersheba (v23-25). *Beersheba* means 'well of the oath', for God had confirmed His covenant with them there.

It was at Beersheba that the Lord actually appeared to them and audibly repeated the words of the covenant. They had found the real presence of God and received revelation from His mouth. It was worth all the effort!

Finally, it was at Beersheba that they set up another camp; they dwelt in the presence of God at the place where His word went forth. They enjoyed all the water they could drink, they were thoroughly blessed and they worshipped God. Their old enemy, Abimelech, could only say one thing, *'We see plainly that the Lord has been with you'* (v28).

7

Seek the Lord Earnestly

A passionate engagement with God

STEP 5 – I shall seek thee EARNESTLY (Psalm 63:1)

I have never dug a well but I know that to do so would be very hard work. Once a well has been dug there is an abundance of water that will continue for the life of the well, subject to regular maintenance. But to reach the water table takes a lot of time and effort.

> *'And you shall love the Lord your God with all your heart with all your soul and with all your might.'*
>
> (Deuteronomy 6:5)

Heart, soul, might is a way of saying our whole person. Our spirit, our mind and our body; every part of us should be involved in seeking God. Now this does not mean that you have to dance round the room to involve your body – although you may if you wish – it means that the whole of your being is involved in worship.

An unpalatable spiritual truth is that it is not easy to seek God earnestly. It takes discipline, consistency and, as we have seen, will-power. It takes the help of the Holy Spirit and lots of determination to plumb the depths of God, but the rewards are infinite.

Motivation
I have more to say about effort later – I want to go beyond just effort to look at what motivates us to effort. The greatest achievements of man are born of passion. In Psalm 103 when

David says, *'Bless the Lord, O my soul, and all that is within me,'* he is speaking from an inner passion. His spirit is hungry, he is desperate, so hungry for God. It is this passion, tinged with desperation, that breaks through into the realm where God dwells.

This is also the essence of Psalm 63:1:

> *'My soul thirsts for Thee, my flesh yearns for Thee,*
> *In a dry and weary land where there is no water.'*

This inner passion, this yearning, is a cry from deep within to the heart of God. It says, 'I've got to have you, I'm so desperate, come near, my Lord.' Our inner man aches so much, it almost hurts. When our first child was born I used to count the minutes so I could get home and hold her in my arms. I remember once in the garden of our Sydney home consciously experiencing the genuine 'ache' of the love of a father for his children for the first time. Since then my love for my two beautiful children has never diminished but rather increased as my relationship with them has grown. In Ecclesiastes 3:11 Solomon tells us that God has set eternity in our hearts. We need to allow our eternal inner man to break forth through every fibre of our beings. In Psalm 23 David goes beyond his spirit – it is his soul, his mental and emotional being and his flesh, or physical being, that are crying out. The hunger of his spirit is not crushed by his 'flesh' but his flesh is a channel for the deep spiritual hunger that only God can satisfy. In some ways this relates to what we have already said about praying unceasingly, our whole being focused on the Living God.

You will find Him

The passionate, fervent heart will always find God. He wants you to locate Him, but He also wants to feel the 'heat' coming from you:

> *'You will seek Me and find Me, when you search for Me with*
> *all your heart. And I will be found by you...'.*
>
> (Jeremiah 29:13-14)

Be a passionate lover of God!

STEP 6 – Thus I have Beheld You in Your Sanctuary (Psalm 63:2)

The sanctuary is the Holy of Holies, the very dwelling place of God. There was a Holy of Holies in the tabernacle in the wilderness, and the glory of God came into it, and God spoke to the High Priest on behalf of the people – but this is not what David is referring to. It is to the Tabernacle of David on Mount Zion (2 Samuel 6:17), where the ark of the covenant rested.

Having been ousted from Jerusalem into the Judean wilderness by his wicked son Absalom, David reflects in Psalm 63 on the God he has seen face-to-face in the sanctuary on Zion. He conjectures – 'If I can experience God in the sanctuary, then why not out here in the desert?'

There was a heavenly sanctuary that did not depend upon physical location, but as with Jacob at Bethel, it was the spiritual location that was important.

The spiritual location of God's presence is available to each of us, anywhere, any time.

> *'... and the Spirit lifted me up and brought me into the inner court; and behold, the glory of God filled the house.'*
>
> (Ezekiel 43:5)

See

David 'beheld' the Lord in the sanctuary. To 'behold' is to 'see'. We do not know how David actually saw, whether it was a vision to his natural eyes or to his spirit, the important thing is that he 'saw'.

Thirty four times in Scripture the glory of God is 'seen'. Isaiah said, *'I saw the Lord sitting on the throne.'*

Most of us do not have the privilege of seeing spiritual things with our natural eyes, but all of us can see with our spiritual eyes. How sad that we usually walk around with our spiritual 'eyes' shut. If we went through a day with our physical eyes closed we would spend much of it injuring ourselves. If we were shut in a place with absolutely no light we would become frightened of what might lurk in the unseen realm around us. Yet many of us live this way spiritually. One of the reasons Jesus opened so many blind eyes was to show the Jews that they were spiritually blind and needed to see.

Elisha was surrounded by a huge Aramean army, his servant was terrified until Elisha asked the Lord to open his eyes. Suddenly the young man saw, not the vast Aramean army, but the infinitely greater Host of Heaven. He was immediately reassured, the fear left, he became confident and bold.

Visualising

We need to develop our inner seeing faculty. Many people misunderstand this to mean some New Age visualisation process. This New Age concept is nothing but a perversion of God's truth, as so many lies of the devil are.

Most often we think in pictures, not words; we also dream in pictures. Pictures are God's most usual way of communicating to our inner man. When we read the Scriptures we see pictures. Try reading the story of feeding the 5,000 or crossing the Red Sea or the good Samaritan without creating a visual representation in the eye of your mind. It is like watching a movie inside our heads. Pictures are the language of the spirit. Most believers who prophesy will admit that they often see a visual impression which God gives them words to interpret. With the Holy Spirit's help we can begin to develop our seeing faculties and enter into the realm of the spirit.

In the hustle and bustle of everyday life we have lost our ability to see in the spirit. One way to regain it is to invite the Holy Spirit to join you on a pictorial spiritual journey when you next read the 'word'. I challenge you to go further than you ever have before. If it is a narrative, see the characters – their faces, clothing, the colours; see the dust, the palm trees, the rocks, smell the food, enter right into the lives of the people. Feel, see, touch.

STEP 7 – To See Your Power and Your Glory (Psalm 63:2)

A step on from seeing narratives is to read scriptures such as

Isaiah 6:1-4. Let us look at it again briefly:

> *'In the year of King Uzziah's death, I saw the Lord sitting on a throne, lofty and exalted with the train of His robe filling the temple. Seraphim stood above Him, each having six wings; with two he covered his face, and with two he covered his feet and with two he flew. And one called out to another and said, "Holy, Holy, Holy is the Lord of hosts, The whole earth is full of His glory." And the foundations of the thresholds trembled at the voice of him who called out while the temple was filling with smoke.'* (Isaiah 6:1-4)

There is so much to see in this description. Jesus on the throne – what was the throne like? See the train of his robe and the glory of God filling the temple – touch it, touch the seraphim, smell the burning coals. Enter into the realm of God's glory. Step by step ask the Holy Spirit to show you, to reveal things to you. This will revolutionise not only your Bible reading but your praise and worship, prayer life and ministry. Soon you will be able to see in the spirit and enter into the realm of God's presence in a way you had not even dreamed of.

Be transformed

Romans 12:2 exhorts us to be transformed by the renewing of our minds. As we develop the way we 'see', our mind will dwell on the things of the spirit and we will be transformed.

In every situation we will begin to see God's power and glory. We will begin, like Bezalel, to be a craftsman in the spirit (Exodus 31:3).

God builds on our thoughts

Living in the spirit does not mean we only think about thrones, angels and visions of heaven. Sometimes we can be thinking about something mundane and God can turn it into a fully fledged vision. In Acts chapter 10, Peter was staying at a tanner's house. Now this wasn't a very good place for a devout Jew to be,

48

because a tanner was involved with dead animals and was permanently unclean. Peter went onto the roof to pray. While he was praying he became hungry and, thinking about food, he may have started to feel guilty about staying in such a place and eating there. This gave God an opening to bring a vision of clean and unclean animals to remind Peter that they were all created by God. Initially this vision met the local situation, his staying and eating with Simon the tanner, but God extended the context of the vision to include Gentile believers and to prepare him for a visit from Cornelius' servant. All this developed from some worrying thoughts in Peter's mind.

So much of what the Holy Spirit says we do not even listen to, but it is possible to become razor sharp in our perceptions and our relationship with God can develop dramatically. Most of us live very unsatisfactory spiritual lives but the sky is the limit as we begin to seek the opportunities presented to us by the Holy Spirit.

8

Entering In

Taking God's presence captive, a violent act!

'Now the King and his men went to Jerusalem against the Jebusites, the inhabitants of the land, and they said to David, "You shall not come in here, but the blind and lame shall turn you away;" thinking, "David cannot enter here." Nevertheless, David captured the stronghold of Zion, that is the city of David. And David said on that day, "Whoever would strike the Jebusites, let him reach the lame and the blind, who are hated by David's soul, through the water tunnel." Therefore they say, "The blind and the lame shall not come into the house." So David lived in the stronghold and called it the city of David ...' (2 Samuel 5:6-9)

"You shall not come in here, but the blind and lame shall turn you away;" thinking David cannot enter here.
(2 Samuel 5:6)
Repeatedly in Scripture Mount Zion represents the dwelling place of God's presence:

'But you have come to Mount Zion and to the city of the living God, the heavenly Jerusalem, and to myriads of angels.' (Hebrews 12:22)

Zion became the dwelling place of King David, where the Ark of the Covenant rested, and where later King Solomon would build the magnificent temple. As far as the Scriptures are concerned Mount Zion and Jerusalem are synonymous terms.

As David approached the stronghold of Zion the enemy taunted him saying, *'You shall not come in here, but the blind and lame shall turn you away.'* In the same way the enemy will taunt you about coming into God's presence.

Zion was called Jebus at the time of David's attack. It was a natural rock fortress that had withstood every enemy attack. Even going back to the days of Joshua, it had never been possessed by any of the tribes of Israel. It was a wicked place, inhabited by wicked people – yet after David took it it became, and remains, the most significant religious capital on the earth.

You see there is hope for our cities however wicked they are. God can turn them around as his people rise up in the spirit of faith, like David.

The Jebusites had become complacent, they felt so secure in their natural fortress that they taunted their enemies – even our lame and blind (our weakest) can keep your strongest at bay. Christians have been so weak for so long that the devil has become secure and let his guard down. A half-decent attack from the Church in this hour would send him running. It's a psychological war. In reality Satan does not have a grip at all. As long as he can convince us that we are wasting our time he will keep the upper hand – so he taunts us about our weaknesses and reminds us of his strength. He reminds us that we have not prayed enough, that our marriages are not good enough, that we have not told an unbeliever about Jesus lately or that we lose our temper, or get jealous – or he suggests a whole catalogue of other misdemeanours.

The irony is that the very things that we allow to keep us out of God's presence are the reason we should be in it. We overcome the flesh by the spirit, not by the flesh.

Some preachers and so-called prophets join the voices against us – God can't move until you repent, put this right, go up to that person, pray an hour a day – conditions, tons of them! What about grace? What about God's ability to break into our world and touch our lives again? Our achievement, good works and victory over sin are by the spirit. I want this book to liberate you, not intimidate you. The Holy Spirit does not intimidate, threaten or condemn – He is the Spirit of life in Christ Jesus; He has set us free!

Don't listen to the Jebusite spirit saying, *'You shall not come in here...'* (2 Samuel 5:6) because it is a lie; you can enter! You can do all things through Christ – if God is for you, who can be against you? Do we agree with Satan or with Jesus? Arise and possess your inheritance!

Nevertheless, David captured the stronghold (2 Samuel 5:7).

I like the next word in this narrative – 'Nevertheless'. In other words, 'Whatever you say, Devil, may be naturally true, but I live in spiritual truth. Despite your taunts I will capture this stronghold; I will embrace the presence of God.' David wasn't the sort to submit to a taunt. It had not been all that long since David stood before Goliath the Philistine who was full of taunts. Goliath disdained David for being too young: *'Am I a dog that you come to me with sticks?' 'Come to me and I will give your flesh to the birds of the sky and the beasts of the field.'* (1 Samuel 17:43-44).

This should have terrified 'little' David. Maybe it did, but he certainly wasn't showing it. *'You come to me with a sword, a spear, and a javelin, but I come to you in the Name of the Lord of Hosts, the God of the armies of Israel whom you have taunted,'* he retaliated (v45). The armies of Israel had responded to the taunts in the way so many of us have, but David, smaller than most, had the courage to listen to God rather than man or the devil:

> *'This day the Lord will deliver you into my hands and I will strike you down and remove your head from you. And I will give the dead bodies of the army of the Philistines this day to the birds of the sky and the wild beasts of the earth, that all the earth may know that there is a God in Israel, and that all this assembly may know that the Lord does not deliver by sword or by spear, for the battle is the Lord's and He will give you into our hands.'* (1 Samuel 17:46-47)

Rather than being intimidated by taunts we need to remind our enemy about the power of the shed blood of Jesus and the victory of the Cross.

Through the water tunnel (2 Samuel 5:8).

I am convinced that this portion of Scripture was given to us, among other things, to show us how to capture the presence of God. This was not a full frontal assault; David entered the city in a way that no-one had ever done before; through a water tunnel.

This tunnel was later to receive improvement under King Hezekiah. Hezekiah's tunnel was one of the wonders of the ancient world, taking water from the Springs of Gihon all the way into the Pool of Siloam in the centre of Jerusalem.

Breaking forth

The waters of Gihon are 'living waters' representing the Holy Spirit; Gihon means 'breaking forth', thus it is through the water tunnel we break forth against our enemies and into the presence of God.

I like to use the word 'propelled'; it is as if David's army stepped into the spirit and was propelled against the enemy into the heart of Zion. Incredibly, the word *Siloam* means 'as a missile that is sent' – we can launch into the heart of God's presence like a missile as this revelation sinks into our hearts.

Breaking forth in the spirit is more than speaking out the 'word', it is more than following principles, or having the right attitude, it is even more than doing the right thing – it is living in a different dimension, the world of the Holy Spirit.

The Bible says we do not war in the flesh but in the Spirit (2 Corinthians 10:3-6) and that the letter kills but the Spirit gives life (2 Corinthians 3:6). Jesus said, *'It is the Spirit who gives life; the flesh profits nothing'* (John 6:63).

It is time to act, to take hold of the things of the spirit and arise in power! Be violent! *'...The kingdom of heaven suffers violence, and violent men take it by force'* (Matthew 11:12). The things of God are to be seized hold of violently. Our flesh must respond to the Spirit. Have you ever noticed that when you don't feel like doing something – dancing, clapping, running, speaking to someone, or even doing a task – and then make the effort, it somehow liberates? A good example of this is prayer. When we put real physical effort into our prayer, we step into the spirit of prayer. Personally I find it very difficult to reach this place while

53

sitting still in a chair, I have to get up and get into it! Usually when I pray loudly and move my body there will follow a time of stillness as the presence of God falls. The shouts turn to whispers, any form of movement seems sacrilege. This is God's quiet; it means we have taken possession of Zion – it is not a mind-wandering fidgety quiet, it is a pregnant quiet, full of the birthings of God, revelation and glory.

I repeat, it takes effort, but we are built for it! Joshua had to drive out the giants from Canaan, David had to drive out the Jebusites; we too must rise up against the spiritual giants that stand before us.

9

Do It God's Way

Getting spiritually smart

Even Jesus was involved in a tension between His ways and His Father's ways. When He was in the Garden of Gethsemene facing His greatest test He wrestled in prayer before conceding, *'Yet not My will, but Thine be done'* (Luke 22:42).

David's success depended upon his willingness and ability to hear and obey the word of the Lord. Our spiritual warfare often fails because we neglect to concede that it is spiritual; *'... we do not war according to the flesh, for the weapons of our warfare are not of the flesh...'* (2 Corinthians 10:3-4). Before going to war against spiritual enemies we need to know what God is saying about it. Is the time right? Should I bind the devil or sing praises to God? Revelation is essential! Before returning to our biblical narrative on the capture of Zion (in chapter 10), we will take a closer look at this important topic.

The spoken word

There is a difference between the two Greek words both translated 'word' in the Bible – *rhema* and *logos*. Every word in the Bible is the true *logos* of God. *Logos* is Greek, meaning 'the word', *rhema* is Greek for the 'spoken word'. For instance, before facing the Philistines, David prayed, *'Shall I go up against the Philistines? Will thou give them into my hand?'* (2 Samuel 5:19).

David already had the *logos* word to drive out the Philistines:

> *'Speak to the sons of Israel and say to them, "When you cross over' the Jordan into the land of Canaan, then you shall drive out all the inhabitants of the land from before*

55

This word gave David the general authority, but he needed specific revelation for this situation; this is why his prayer was so important.

You and I have authority over every demon in the Name of Jesus, but this doesn't mean we can simply stand alone against satanic powers in the Name of the Lord and expect them to leave meekly. We need to know God's current agenda in a particular situation. Warfare is a precise science, not a haphazard affair.

Hearing from God

When I first came to London in 1987 I went on some very long fasts and stood against the powers of London alone, marching up and down the streets and taking authority. Much of what I did produced results, I know. Yet I personally experienced extreme spiritual backlash.

I learned to wait, to seek God about a situation before going to war. I slowly became more God-conscious and less devil-conscious. I continued to walk the streets praying, praising and releasing the presence of God and I began to receive the *rhema* word.

One day I was having a terrible time. After a period of fasting, I walked all the way round the square mile of London, then transversed it from north to south and east to west. The heavens were like 'brass' as I prayed – even one single 'hallelujah' was desperately hard to find. Tired and very hungry I boarded the tube for home. Then quietly the Lord spoke to my heart, 'Bring the whole church and march around the city with singers and musicians.'

At that time, I was pastor of a West London church called Christian City Church. We had great musicians. The Australia-based CCC movement produced some marvellous praise and warfare songs in the 1980's such as 'We have a vision for this nation' and 'Rise up, you people of power'. As we marched we knew the Holy Spirit was flowing through us. On every corner we stopped to pray and praise the Lord. The heavens were open, the tangible presence of God was everywhere. We concluded our march at the Roman Wall at Tower Hill and such a weight of glory fell that we just stood still and silent in a large circle with hands lifted up. We knew we had done something major in the spirit but it was in response to a *rhema* word; we were enjoying the fruit of obedience.

A scripture that has always meant a lot to me is something Jesus said in John's gospel:

> *'... the Son can do nothing of Himself, unless it is something He sees the Father doing; for whatever the Father does, these things the Son also does in like manner.'* (John 5:19)

At Metropolitan College of Ministry, in London, where I serve as principal, we have a reputation for powerful prayer which involves destroying enemy strongholds over the city. Sometimes we will pray for some weeks before getting a strategy or attacking a particular enemy in a particular way. We realize the need for hearing from God in every situation and we will just continue to pray, mainly in tongues, until He speaks. We must see what the Father is doing, then do likewise.

His angel will go before us

> *'For My angel will go before you and bring you in to the land of the Amorites, the Hittites, the Perizzites, the Canaanites, the Hivites and the Jebusites; and I will completely destroy them.'* (Exodus 23:23)

There is a strong angel in the presence of the Lord who stands with us whenever we are in the spirit. The angel will prevail against our enemies so we get assured victory. He will also protect us from every attack – *'And the angel of His presence saved them'* (Isaiah 63:9) – dare we go into battle without the heavenly hosts?

> *'Bless the Lord, you His angels,*
> *Mighty in strength who perform His word,*

Obeying the voice of His word!
Bless the Lord, all you His hosts,
You who serve Him, doing His will.'   (Psalm 103:20-21)

When we are in the presence of the Living God we know what to do and when to do it, and that all the resources of heaven are with us. Too many of us either charge into battle without the first bit of direction from the Lord, or else we allow ourselves to be spiritually oppressed, so we avoid the fight altogether. I praise God for the major prophetic move in the Church of the nineties. It is enabling us to receive direction and understanding of the times, empowering us to move in current spiritual truth; not in yesterday's revelation, but in an up-to-the-minute appraisal of the situations we face. The devil and demons don't live in the past, they are up with the latest worldly trends. There is an urgency for us to find the Lord in every situation – we need to get spiritually smart.

The devil has great power

It may shock you to realize that even the smallest demon is more powerful than you. You have no ability to stand against them and win. It is only through the work of the Cross and the authority given to us that we can overpower the enemy. Outside of the Holy Spirit's power we are impotent. In the spirit we have God and all His resources on our side – *'and the God of peace will soon crush Satan under your feet'* (Romans 16:20). They may be our feet but it is God who does the crushing!

The Holy Spirit is with us in battle

To win our spiritual battles, to pull down the enemy strongholds, to have victory, we have to be in the spirit. We get a good biblical picture of this in the book of Isaiah – *'Rise up, captains, oil the shields'* (Isaiah 21:5). This was a trained, disciplined army, in battle array, ready for war. The shields of the captains represent faith, '... *taking up the shield of faith with which you will be able to extinguish all the flaming missiles of the evil one'* (Ephesians 6:16). Brother Lawrence relates faith to the presence of God thus:

> 'The first benefit that the soul receives from the presence of God, is that faith becomes more alive and active in all the processes of our life.'[1]

The first thing we see is the need to keep our faith 'oiled'. Oil in Scripture refers to the Holy Spirit. So many search for faith in the flesh, attempting some form of mind over matter, but true faith is born of the Holy Spirit and the word of God. Faith is trust and trust is built by relationship. Relationship is built by being with someone and communicating with them. Let us look at some other aspects of the oil and the shield.

Oil polishes | The surface of the shield becomes slippery and deflects arrows, or as our Ephesians verse tells us, *'all the flaming missiles of the evil one.'* Our shield of faith, properly oiled, will protect us from all the schemes of the devil.

Oil prevents deterioration | Have you ever put your finger through rusty metal? A rusty shield is useless. The oil protects our shield of faith from the deterioration of doubt. Faith that is built of the Spirit and the 'word' will never fail.

Oil shines | The surface of the shield will catch the light and blind the enemy; particularly as the enemy lives in darkness. The light is the word of God, and the Glory of God. It will throw our spiritual enemies into disarray and defeat.

Finally, an oiled shield is always ready. We don't wait for difficulties before taking up the shield of faith – as Christians we

[1]Ibid., p76.

are always in battle array with shields well oiled and at hand. Being in the presence of God is our position for war.

10

Living in the Presence of God

Not a visitor, a resident. God's presence is 'home'

So David lived in the stronghold (2 Samuel 5:9)
The fact that you are reading this book indicates that you are a person who hungers for God. What a difference we could make in this world if we lived in the presence of God just like David lived in the stronghold of Zion.

As we have seen in the book of Ezekiel, the Lord took the prophet into the waters of the Spirit until he could not stand on the riverbed:

> *'When the man went out towards the east with a line in his hand, he measured a thousand cubits, and he led me through the water, water reaching the ankles. Again he measured a thousand and led me through the water, water reaching the knees. Again he measured a thousand and led me through the water, water reaching the loins. Again he measured a thousand; and it was a river I could not ford.'*
>
> (Ezekiel 47:3-5)

The 'man' who led Ezekiel through the waters, into the presence of God, measured a thousand cubits at a time. Each one of these thousand cubit measures is a dimension of the Spirit. We see the term 'measure' elsewhere in Scripture in regard to faith:

> *'... as God has allotted to each a measure of faith.'*
>
> (Romans 12:3)

We have heard a lot of teaching about what can be done with the smallest measure of faith. I think a mustard seed of faith is poverty rations. Jesus never congratulated anyone for having a little bit of faith, only when they had great faith.

A mustard seed of faith is not what moves the mountain, it is what a mustard seed becomes as it is grown in the right conditions. The power in the seed is latent. I want exceeding great faith!

We enter into the presence of God by faith

> *'Therefore I say to you, all things for which you pray and ask, believe you have received them, and they shall be granted you.'* (Mark 11:24)

This is how I received the baptism in the Holy Spirit (Chapter 1) and this is also how we grow in the spirit and dwell in God's presence. It is simple, just believe you are already there!

Faith is always tested. Remember the difficulties Jacob faced when he found water in the wells he had dug (Genesis 26:19-21). If we prove faithful in the first one thousand cubits and do not shrink back we will enter the second. God is very precise, He has a measuring rod. It takes a little more faith to go in and stay in up to our knees and still more faith to go in up to our loins.

Live in the river

Ezekiel tells us that wherever the river went everything lived (v9). There is no death in God's river, leaves will not whither and fruit will not fail. We should always be filled with the Holy Spirit, enjoying God's presence to the full.

The presence of God is not just the feeling we get in church, at homegroup, in the prayer meeting, or sometimes when we pray. It is a place! Not a place to visit, a place to stay. It is home!

> *'I will dwell in the house of the Lord forever.'* (Psalm 23:6)

This is the place Jacob visited, even though 'in the natural' he was in the midst of a desert:

'This is none other than the house of God, and this is the gate of heaven.' (Genesis 28:17)

What then is the house of God? It is where His presence is; the spirit realm.

When Mary and Joseph could not find young Jesus He turned up in the most obvious place, the temple. His words to them should be the cry of our hearts too, *'Did you not know that I had to be in My Father's house?'* (Luke 2:49) . The same chapter in Luke (v37) says the prophetess Anna, *'never left the temple, serving night and day with fasting and prayers.'*

Always in His presence

When we are in the spirit we are in the house of God. We sense His presence all the time and release His presence wherever we go. The Holy Spirit penetrates every fibre of our being. Many of the things we have striven for in the past start to come to us easily. The trees in Ezekiel 47:12 were therapeutic, for healing; also in Revelation 22:2 the Greek *therapeia* translates healing. When the Spirit of God permeates our lives we will walk in health, renewed physical strength, and vigour.

Finally, we will radiate His glory. Peter, in the book of Acts, carried such a presence that people were healed by his shadow. Paul's handkerchief was filled with the glory of God and people were healed as they touched it. Many of the great men and women of God of the twentieth century carry such a weight of glory that people fall under the power of God when they get near them – even in hotel foyers, railway carriages and other public places, without a word being spoken. You can never be another Wigglesworth, Kuhlman or Hinn but you can be the real you. We have not even begun to realize what God will do in our lives when we seek Him with our whole being, stepping into His glorious presence and remaining there.

Changing the 'atmosphere'

From a position in God's presence we have the ability to change the spiritual atmosphere around us, in our homes, workplaces, wherever God puts us. We can influence the atmosphere of our city as we release God's presence through its streets and market places. The 'feel' of churches can be revolutionised as believers pray through the auditorium, releasing the presence of God, creating an environment for praise, worship, powerful preaching, prophecy, salvation and healing:

> *'I will dwell in the house of the Lord forever.'*   (Psalm 23:6)

I pray you have been challenged and helped by this book and that you are already feeling closer to God. May He draw you into the close communion of His presence and may you abide in the secret places of the Most High God forever.

❖   ❖   ❖   ❖

If you have enjoyed this book and would like to help us to send a copy of it and many other titles to needy pastors in the **Third World**, please write for further information or send your gift to:

Sovereign World Trust, P.O. Box 777, Tonbridge, Kent TN11 9XT, United Kingdom

or to the **'Sovereign World'** distributor in your country. If sending money from outside the United Kingdom, please send an International Money Order or Foreign Bank Draft in STERLING, drawn on a **UK** bank to **Sovereign World Trust**.